A MANIFESTO FROM AN OPEN HEART ♡

PATHWAYS TO LIVING AUTHENTICALLY

SAULAN BEVERLY YIN-LO

Testimonials

Saulan provided me with a safe and open space to share thoughts, experiences and insight. She had a genuine interest in what I had to say which allowed me to feel heard and understood. The insight she provided was very useful to my everyday life and allowed me to look at my current situation from a different perspective. She supported me to see my inner potential which I will always be grateful for.

Lukkas Buchler

It was truly an amazing experience working with Saulan as her client for the past 6 weeks. Saulan's gentle, encouraging, insightful and committed approach provided me with a safe and nurturing space in which to explore a long lost dream.

Her great skilful techniques enabled me to unpack the many blocks I had, which gently assisted me to move through them. I particularly loved the way she allowed me to see how my passion, purpose and values were intrinsically connected to my goal, this amazingly propelled and fast tracked me over many of my blocks.

In such a short time, I was able to turn a goal that was so remote into a project that is happening. I believe

Saulan has found her passion and purpose in this work. Saulan effortlessly has the ability to skilfully and intuitively take you on a journey of self discovery.

Anna Masella

I have felt so honoured to have been coached by Saulan. Her warmth, perceptions and her genuinely open and giving heart, coupled with her coaching knowledge helped me to achieve very quick and impactful results that I have maintained.

Her ongoing support and ability to seamlessly connect with me made my experience of working with her enjoyable and easy! I highly recommend Saulan.

Fiona Pace-Atienza

I am so thankful for the changes I've made while working with Saulan. I have especially found benefit from the focusing "felt sense" exercise that we have been doing where I have been able to move from feeling confusion and pressure in my head as I function on autopilot, to enjoying peace and calm. I was able to reconnect my mind, heart and spirit so that I can now experience unity as my whole self is on board to live my purpose each day with gratitude.

Wendy Ventura

With insightful sensory perception, listening skill and empathy, Saulan guided me to positive self talk and simple actions for living in and appreciating the 'now'.

Coleen Greene

It's hard to put into words the positive effect that Saulan's life coaching has had on me. She truly is a remarkable woman with an uncanny intuition. 2 months ago, I would never have imagined that I would be in the mindset that I now find myself in. This is all thanks to Saulan and her guidance and encouragement in my future path. Saulan has given me fresh insight as to what was holding me back and I always walk away from our sessions feeling physically taller and mentally stronger. I genuinely don't believe that I would feel so empowered and optimistic towards my goals and even everyday life without Saulan's influence. I'm so appreciative that I received coaching sessions from Saulan and I will ensure that I continue to use the tools that she has given me to make the changes in my life that I choose.

Natasha Thoma

I have worked with Saulan for the past few months and I feel privileged to have her as a coach. Saulan has helped me get clarity with my business and how to live a life of purpose and meaning. She is part strategist, part thought provoker, and part cheerleader.

And she has a masterful knack for knowing when to invoke these various skills to bring out a clarity of purpose and desire that is often hard to pinpoint on your own. She has a way of repackaging your own, sometimes confusing, thoughts in a way that adds meaningful direction. I am also blessed with Saulan's ongoing compassion, wisdom, and graciousness which are a wonderful model for anyone at any time. I could go on and on with superlatives, but suffice to say, I'd wholeheartedly recommend Saulan to anyone looking to take their life to the next level and realise their full potential.

Neil Ferro

A MANIFESTO FROM AN OPEN HEART ♡

PATHWAYS TO LIVING AUTHENTICALLY

SAULAN BEVERLY YIN-LO

Published by the Power Writers Publishing Group in 2023.

Saulan Beverly Yin-Lo © 2023.

All Rights Reserved. No part of this book may be reproduced by any mechanical, photographic, or electronic processes, or in the form of a phonographic recording. Nor may it be stored in a retrieval system, transmitted or otherwise be copied for public or private use other than for 'fair use' - as brief quotations embodied in articles and reviews, without prior written permission of the publisher.

ISBN: 978-0-6456271-8-3 (pbk)

A catalogue record for this book is available from the National Library of Australia

ISBN: 978-0-6458010-0-2 (ebk)

Cover and internal layout by Publicious Book Publishing
www.publicious.com.au

Back cover photograph by Andrew Parkee ©

Disclaimer
Any opinions expressed in this work are exclusively those of the author and are not necessarily the views held or endorsed by others quoted throughout. All of the information, exercises and concepts contained within the publication are intended for general information only. The author does not take any responsibility for any choices that any individual or organization may make in relation to this information in the business, personal, financial, familial or other areas of life based on the choice to use this information. If any individual or organization does wish to implement the ideas discussed herein, it is recommended they obtain their own independent advice specific to their circumstances.

This book is available in print and eBook formats

CONTENTS

PREFACE i

CHAPTER 1: Life Out of my Yellow Bubble 1
CHAPTER 2: Anxiety 9
CHAPTER 3: New Horizons 19
CHAPTER 4: Values and Beliefs 29
CHAPTER 5: Fulfilment and Joy 37
CHAPTER 6: Purpose 47
CHAPTER 7: Emotional Mastery 57
CHAPTER 8: Fun and Travel 67
CHAPTER 9: Self Leadership 77
CHAPTER 10: Relationships 89

CONCLUSION 101
REFERENCES 102
ABOUT THE AUTHOR 103

PREFACE

" Polish from the inside, to shine on the outside"

Saulan

This book is an offering to you by way of a window into what shaped me to want to look beyond everyday existence through trusting that there is more to life than the activity we see around us. My willingness, courage, and curiosity to understand myself is the driving force that has been my constant companion on the road less travelled.

My approach is based on focus, flow and flourishing in mind, body, and spirit. This has taken me on a path of adventure, love, and a deepening sense of clarity around my identity. It opened the door to many more intuitive opportunities and infinite possibilities than I would have been able to discover without it.

Some say we are never dealt with more than we can handle, yet there were times when I questioned that, but if there's one thing I've learnt on this journey called life, it's that nobody but me has control over my mindset and attitude. That's the realisation that made the difference for me.

Owning all the material things we could possibly want is not the answer for me. I say that because it's my attitude that is the key to the level of fulfillment that my positive mind has created. This book is my way of sharing the parts of my journey that taught me that my attitude is the thing that grounds me and motivates me to continue to learn, grow and be authentic in order to live a positive life where I can contribute to the wellbeing of others through the work I do.

I developed five simple pillars that I use to guide me through my life. These came out of the things I learnt during the course of my transformation that played out over decades. I'd encourage you to consider these pillars in relation to your own life as you read the **Thoughts to Steer Your Life With** prompts that you'll find at the end of each chapter. The pillars are:

- Self Awareness
- Mindfulness
- Purpose
- Connection
- Self Care.

You'll find pages at the end of each chapter to write down your reflections on the material you're reading. Among other things, you might find it useful to add in any additional "Thoughts to Steer Your Life With" that come to mind as you reflect on the ones that I've provided.

I'm grateful you've decided to join me by reading this book so that you can become the wonderful true being that you are meant to be. I'm hoping you will be inspired to look within and be able to make a difference to your life and others with the insight you gain through reflecting on what I'm sharing with you here.

CHAPTER 1: Life Out of my Yellow Bubble
"Our life is what our thoughts make it"
Saulan

Leaving my mum's apron's strings was the beginning of an ever-changing life with no end. I was just five years old at the time. It's an understatement in the extreme to say that it felt devastating to enter the big world outside of my 'safe haven' that felt like a beautiful big yellow bubble.

Growing up in a Chinese family where my father didn't speak English and my mother was bilingual, set me up to have a confused mind and feel terribly disoriented when I started moving out of my safety zone.

I think it's fair to say that my way of coping back then was through a psychological process called 'internalisation'. Essentially, internalisation is a deep form of conformity. What this led to as I was growing up was a pretty wobbly sense of myself where I never really felt like I belonged.

I am a baby boomer who was born in 1951. I was the baby of the family until I was five when my little sister came along. I don't know whether I ever really got over the fact that she died at the age of three. I have two older sisters who were reasonably close. My oldest sister was very responsible. She helped Mum and Dad run a small Chinese restaurant, and she was the one who looked after us when Mum and Dad were working at night. My second sister who was between me and my oldest sister was a sick child with asthma. My Paw-Paw (which means grandmother in Chinese) often looked after her because Mum was always busy working.

My sister's behaviour was very unpredictable. Sometimes she would be playful and friendly, then the next minute she would be picking a fight or bullying me if I was a bit teary or showing that I was missing my Mum. I was a 'mummy's girl' which probably created the tension between us. I remember people always comparing us in terms of our looks in particular. I was more on the chubby side and she was light-framed. The family's Chinese friends would often pinch my cheek and say, 'So cute'. I would curtly smile back as I rubbed my cheek. As well as asthma, my sister also had eczema, which is a skin problem she had on her face, arms and legs. She was really self-conscious about that. In hindsight I can see that it wasn't easy for her, yet there wasn't really anything I could do to help.

As children often do, I took everything personally and became very timid. I used to avoid confrontation at any cost. This meant that I wouldn't/couldn't stand up for myself when I was young. Meanwhile, I was very good at accommodating the needs of others. This tendency has more or less followed me like a shadow through most of my life. In fact, acquiescing was my way of managing my interactions with others for decades.

This tendency to always accommodate the needs of others had an impact on my health that showed up when I was the ripe old age of eight. The form it showed up in was anxiety and stress. In fact, emotionally I was a bit of a stressed-out mess as a result of my experience of growing up and developing as a teenager in the Western world with my Chinese values and beliefs that were at odds with the society I was living in. Not to mention the impact of looking different and feeling a none too subtle pressure arising from an 'us and them' mentality that made me feel unwelcome in groups where the other members didn't look like me.

High school was the worst time for me in terms of confusion because there were groups of kids who were of Chinese descent from places like Hong Kong, Singapore and Malaysia. These niches weren't particularly welcoming to me either because no one had the same background as me in terms of being born in Australia. I looked like them, but I still didn't fit into any group. I was in a very bad state living with a dark cloud of confusion and a sense of disconnection and not belonging hanging over me during my school years. The safe bubble of the life I knew when I was little was brutally burst, and the build up of stress and anxiety that turned into depression eventually manifested in skin problems.

This felt like life was adding insult to injury and by the age of fifteen I was suffering with an emotionally and physically debilitating skin problem that seriously exacerbated my depression. It makes me sad to remember what it was like when I was fifteen and my insecurities were so unmanageable that I felt like a lost cause. I was so far out of the yellow bubble that used to give me a sense of security when I was little, that I just felt lost and alone in my misery for the last three years of my school life.

Thoughts to Steer Your Life With

- Never give up: Even if you are in an emotional 'fog' and things feel really dark, there is always hope because people like us are resilient.

- Beliefs matter: Holding the intention of achieving something you are aiming for, and maintaining a belief in achieving a positive outcome, will lessen the emotional load you have to carry through the dark times. It is also likely to improve the results that you get.

NOTES

NOTES

NOTES

CHAPTER 2: Anxiety

"You are only confined by the walls you build yourself"

Saulan

My first three years out of school was also a challenging time for me. School had been hard for me and I was expecting to have more control of my life when I left school. To my disappointment I found that there were just as many rules outside of school that didn't suit me, as there were when I was an out of place teenager. Really it was a case of being different, but kind of the same.

Again, I felt lost and alone. I had no idea what the rules for life were, and I was essentially back to square one. My emotional state was still in turmoil, and by this time my inner critic was in overdrive. To sum the situation up, I had well and truly honed the craft of being disconnected from myself by then.

Anxiety was a major theme in my day to day existence back then. It did nothing to help me maintain (or even develop) a healthy relationship with my mind, body, and spirit. All I wanted to be was 'normal' from my own perspective. What that meant to me at the time was being able to fit in with others. The problem was that there was an image in my mind of who I was that made that 'goal' feel like it wasn't possible. With all of that playing out in the back of my mind the waves of anxiety were constantly sweeping in and out, over and under, and forcing me to struggle to keep my head above water with the threat of the wild ocean called 'life' swallowing me up.

At times the sense of powerlessness and hopelessness I felt was overwhelming. I was drowning in my sorrows and out of control. The problem was that I used up all of my energy accommodating people just like I used to do when I was a small child. In retrospect I can see that it wasn't living that I was doing. What I was doing was barely even existing. I say that because I lived in a constant state of fear that I would not be liked; that I was not worthy; and that I had nothing to offer.

There's no question that words are powerful. I can describe the first half of my life using words like pain, nervous breakdown, eczema, mental moods of destruction, guilt, fear, lack of self-esteem, and anger. This toxic soup of words represents what was going on in my mind and my body. Everyone around me seemed to have it all together. Meanwhile I was eating my emotions and scoffing down comfort food as a chaser. I can see now that this was my way of taking my mind off not belonging and constantly questioning if there was any purpose in my life.

Meanwhile the festering allergies I suffered from were erupting all over my skin. I was a mess! At one stage I looked like a character from a horror movie. My face was so swollen that my eyes could hardly open. Luckily for me I worked at a pharmacy and my boss generously gave me tablets to ease the ferocity of the reaction my body was having to my allergies. These tablets made me drowsy, and I would often fall asleep on the bus home. One day I woke up and realised I had missed my stop. That was a turning point for me. It was like a kind of metaphor sent from above.

The message I got was - STOP! It was time to get of this bus that was taking me nowhere. I had a powerful insight at that point that I needed to choose my destination and make a choice to do whatever it takes to get there. I guess it was a simmering sense of self-worth that raised its head (although it didn't feel like it at the time) that lead me to ask myself important questions like - where did I want to be; what is this thing called life all about; what was my purpose?

Reflecting on my journey up to now with particular reference to that turning point, I realise this is what set me on a path that I'm still on today where I challenge myself to be the best version of me I can be, by asking those three important questions. Doing that is how I stay grounded and in a state of equanimity.

It felt like forever as I was waiting to turn seventeen so that I could get into nursing. My dream was to work overseas with children and further my career by specialising in paediatrics or obstetrics. My mind was focused on helping others and providing service in the third world communities that needed it the most.

I started nursing at the Royal Prince Alfred Hospital in Sydney in 1968. Moving out of home and living in the residential area for nurses at the hospital was an adventure for me. I was on my own and being responsible for making choices that would shape the rest of my life. Getting my head around the culture of the hospital and the nurses who enrolled at the same time as I did, was interesting. A lot of the nurses were from country areas such as Maitland and Mudgee, and the others were suburban young women like me. We ate, slept, studied, and worked together, so we learned to be tolerant and supportive of each other. We each had our own basic room with a single bed, a wardrobe, and a desk. This was exciting for me. Among other things, I had never had my own space before. Coming from a family of five girls who were pretty close in age meant that I would never get to see what it was like to not be sharing a room with others until I moved out of home.

I started dating a fellow from Singapore who came to Australia as a student when he was thirteen during my preliminary training. He had been educated in Australia like me, but unlike me, he had no family here. He lived with an Anglo-Saxon Chaplain in the Methodist church and learned to love the English language through the Chaplain's wife. Hooking up with someone who was coming from another perspective engendered a renewed appreciation of the value of our cultural heritage in me. It can be so easy to take things like this for granted. It was not that I was unhappy with my family's heritage. It was that I had difficulty when it came to the integration of both the Chinese and Australian parts of who I was that seemed to haunt me for most of my life.

I expected that falling in love and eventually getting married would stabilise me and give me a sense of belonging, especially as I gave up nursing to have a family and live happily ever after. I had a new identity, a new role as a wife, and a year after that I took up another role as a mother. Finally, having three children of my own provided me with a purpose. Well, at least that's what it felt like back then.

Thoughts to Steer Your Life With

- Maintain flexibility: When you make a plan, remain aware of what's going on around you and be ready to pivot if you see new opportunities or challenges on the horizon.

- Make the most of your mind: Developing a growth mindset and remaining self-aware will position you to succeed on your own terms.

- Everyone matters: Be open to cultural diversity and inclusion, and always look for the best in others.

NOTES

NOTES

NOTES

NOTES

CHAPTER 3: New Horizons

"No-one ever injured their eyesight by looking on the bright side"

Saulan

The way forward was clear, or so I thought.

I say that because in hindsight I know I had my rose-coloured glasses on at this stage. I was ensconced in the business of building family relationships that would help me in the new role of being a mother. Motherhood can be a wonderful experience, and I was in my element growing and learning about being a mother with my first son. It wasn't only all that I thought it would be - it was even better.

In the Chinese custom, the first born being a son brings joy to the extended family. There was no exception in our own case, and we had delighted grandparents and other relatives in Sydney and Singapore who were keen to spend time with our son. In fact, our first trip to meet my in-laws in Singapore in the early seventies was really exciting. The initiation and introduction to my partner's family was quite an eye opener for a suburban Australian-born Chinese girl from Alexandria in the inner city area of Sydney.

My husband's family was considered to be well to do. His father came from Fukkien origins (Fukkien is a Chinese province). He was an entrepreneur and business tycoon with three wives. Two of them lived in the same two storey house and the father alternated between them. The first wife was left in China and the son lived in Singapore. The second wife who was domesticated and took control of the household duties didn't speak English. She only spoke Cantonese. She was a great cook. She was also very pleasant and had four children.

My husband's mother was the typical social and business wife who accompanied her husband on social and business occasions. She spoke English, Mandarin, Malay, Cantonese, and Shanghainese, so she was a great asset to her husband when he was catching up with international business contacts. The house had a couple of amahs. These are Chinese servants who have the duty of performing a variety of jobs in the home, as well as a driver/chauffeur who did all the driving for the family.

Regardless of the deep, rich Asian upbringing and the affluence he grew up around, my husband was humble and appreciated the simple life we lived in Australia. I think he enjoyed the uncomplicated lifestyle of my family with no airs or graces and loads of genuine hospitality with no sense of being judged.

I recall meeting a slightly balding man with a noticeably small stature and a very serious face carrying a pillow under his arm on the stairway the first time I visited my husband's family. I smiled shyly not really knowing who he was. Somehow, he didn't really fit the impression I had of a tycoon. I guess that was because he was dressed in long striped pyjama pants with a drawstring and a soft T-shirt style top. To my surprise, this was my new father-in-law.

My fifteen-month-old son was the first grandson, so he was treated like a little Prince. They all wanted to know what he liked to eat, what he played with, and what they could do to make him happy.

I was keen to be seen as the 'ideal' mother, but despite my strong Chinese heritage, my upbringing in Australia made me quite different to them. Although I knew that it could have been worse for the family because my husband told me that he was warned not to come home with a 'pinky' which is what his parents called Anglo-Saxons. That could have easily been the case because he had left home when he was thirteen to study at a Catholic high school in the Eastern Suburbs of Sydney, and he went on to do his Bachelor of Arts degree at the University of NSW. He could have easily wound up with an Aussie blond under those circumstances. His father wanted him to be a businessman and to do a Master's degree in Business. That never happened though because my husband was a humanities person through and through. I guess that's why we hit it off so well.

Being introduced into a well-to-do Chinese family from Singapore was another learning experience for me. Through it I got a chance to get better at adapting to new situations. We had a friendly chauffeur called Aman who was from Malaysia. He would drop us wherever we wanted to go and wait until we finished sightseeing, shopping or eating the delicacies of the Orient so that he could drive us home. Singapore is well known for its hospitality and the quality of its food.

My husband had been living overseas for decades, so the family was thrilled to be seeing a new generation of the Ch'ng family for the first time, and they treated us accordingly. Here we were living overseas for six weeks in a two-storey mansion. It's an understatement to say that this was a lifestyle I wasn't used to. We were very close to the beach and a beautiful park which was lovely to walk around. We also had the luxury of having our meals cooked by my husband's father's first wife, and servants to wash and clean up, along with being entertained and spoiled by the second wife who was my husband's birth mother. We were chauffeur-driven everywhere like movie stars being taken around Singapore to do some shopping and visit the tourist spots.

We really enjoyed our time away visiting my in-laws. That said, as lovely as it was to indulge in the affluence of their world, it felt good to get back to our own life in our suburban two-bedroom garden flat at the back of an Italian family's house.

Thoughts to Steer Your Life With

- Be adaptable and don't fear change: The only thing that doesn't change is the fact that change happens.

- Be open to learning about yourself and others: Treat cultural diversity and inclusion as an opportunity to learn more about what makes people tick.

- Be grateful for what you have, not what you don't have: It's the small things that make the difference.

NOTES

NOTES

NOTES

NOTES

CHAPTER 4: Values and Beliefs

*"Your habits become your values,
Your values become your destiny"*

Mahatma Gandhi

Self-realisation is a term used in Western psychology, philosophy, and spirituality, as well as in Indian religions. Broadly speaking, the Western understanding of self-realisation is based around the fulfillment of one's potential.

The values and beliefs we grow up with are key to the ease with which we are able to achieve that goal. These are passed down to us as we grow up. In a sense they are embedded within us. Without necessarily knowing it, our values and beliefs are the things that determine the decisions we make. That's why it's worth considering the way your upbringing is showing up in your life as an adult to identify any programming that isn't serving you well anymore.

The culture in my family was all about having a solid work ethic. I guess this was born of the fact that my parents didn't have the luxury of not having to worry about being able to pay the bills like my husband's family could. When I left home and started to be freer in my mindset and attitude, I felt that I needed to have a sense of abundance rather than the deficit model I grew up with, however it took me a while to change my attitude. Fast forward to 2023 and I'm a person who likes to take action on things that matter to me and do the best I can whenever I take something on. I now see the value that I can offer to the broader society as well as to myself.

We would visit my Paw Paw (Grandmother) every Sunday when I was growing up. My mum had seven brothers and one sister. I'll always be grateful for the insights I gained from a couple of my uncles who were young and explorative when it came to finding ways to understand what makes people tick. I was really intrigued by that topic at the time. It was the late 50-60s era when there were no mobile phones or anything like that. In fact, we used to have to leave the house and walk to the red telephone box that had a public telephone in it across the road if we needed to make a call. At my Paw Paw's house where my uncles lived there were all kinds of books and other things that they used for personal development scattered all over the lounge room.

I recall a massive green metal tape recorder with two big reels on it that my uncles used to have. It was a bit like a cassette player but twice the size. It was such a novelty in comparison to my everyday life of going to school where teachers used blackboards and chalk, and kids like me used a pencil and paper. It was also in stark contrast to the small devices most of us have in our pockets these days. It felt like we were the 'guinea pigs' for our uncles to test their theories and new playthings like their tape recorder out on. On the upside, we discovered a lot about our personalities and what our strengths were when we spent time with them.

I can't actually remember what my strengths were back then, but I know they would have been more on the social than the academic side of the equation.

The books my uncles were reading were around personal development, self-help, philosophy, pop culture and the other trends the 70s era is known for. I loved the fact that these were the things my uncles were into, and that they shared what they were learning with their inquisitive nieces. I was fascinated by the magic of it all. These days we hear a lot more about personal development, but in those days my uncles were almost trailblazers reading books like "Think and Grow Rich" by Napoleon Hill, and "Success Through a Positive Mental Attitude" that he wrote with Clement Stone, along with "How to Win Friends and Influence People" by Dale Carnegie.

Just as my uncles were searching for the meaning of life, and honing in on their own purpose when I was just a kid, I'm doing the same now myself. And I want to acknowledge that what my uncles contributed to my education helped me much more than what I learnt from the formal education system that I spent 12 years of my life in.

Thoughts to Steer Your Life With

- Mindset is all important: There is great power in having a positive mantra like - *Day by day I get better and better at what I do and how I show up*.

- Knowledge is power: Don't always believe what you're told. Consider everything through the lens of your values, and never be afraid to ask questions.

- Treat life like a never-ending learning opportunity: Use your mind to think and grow for as long as you're alive.

NOTES

NOTES

NOTES

CHAPTER 5: Fulfillment and Joy

"When the Mind is pure, joy follows like a shadow that never leaves"

Buddha

Breathe in, Breathe out! The simplicity of maintaining a natural consistent breathing pattern can be challenging at times. This is because anxiety and stressful situations can interrupt the natural process of breathing oxygen in and exhaling carbon dioxide out. It's the fact that we are likely to be unaware of our unhealthy behaviour patterns until we become ill that keeps the medical systems in countries like Australia stretched to the limit.

I remember those moments as a teenager when my breathing was short, shallow and fast while I was going to a school where racism and bullying was a daily occurrence for me. My body was screaming at me, telling me that this can't go on, and asking when it was going to be my time to have fulfillment and joy.

It took me a long time to really get to a place where I metaphorically stood up and said to myself that now is my time to shine and enjoy an abundance of joy in my life. My 70th birthday was when I decided it was time for me to show up as ME 'warts and all'. That was my time to expose myself while kicking imposter syndrome to the curb and getting the 'shadow saboteur' out of my life. I had been chipping away at the invisible barriers that had kept me stuck for so long, but it finally hit home that I was as entitled as anyone else to be able to revel in the feeling of pure joy when I left my 60s behind me.

I'll never forget the first time I felt the exhilarating feeling of being truly connected with myself where every part of my body was in alignment. This resulted in the muscles in my face becoming engaged in a way that felt like a big fat smile was spread across my face from ear to ear.

It's crazy how underestimated the importance of breathing well is. I say that because it helps us to slow down and take the pressure off, and it enables us to declutter our mind and gain clarity in our thoughts. So, if you want to dramatically improve the quality of your life, I urge you to breathe in through your nostrils to the count of eight while drawing the air all the way into your belly as you imagine releasing the grey smoke of negativity as you let the breath out. I promise if you do this several times a day (especially before you go to bed), you'll be amazed by how quickly you'll start feeling better.

I often think about what took me so long to reach this point. Basically, what it comes down to is a chronic lack of self-esteem. It was that little voice in the back of my head that convinced me that I would never be good enough to be proud about who I am. With that limiting belief driving the agenda I felt like I was powerless which led me to making excuses, blaming others, procrastination, perfectionism, confusion, and a whole lot of emotional baggage that weighed me down energetically and emotionally. The bottom line was that I wasn't taking personal responsibility for the outcomes I was getting. I only achieved what I was able to achieve back in the bad old days because of my capacity to remain in flow while under stress.

That was ok I guess, but in that state, I achieved a whole lot less than I would have if I was able to access the full extent of my intelligence, creativity, and talents. I'm blessed that I acquired the value of 'never giving up' and the inner strength of my grandmother and mother who were the examples I followed when I was young. I am full of gratitude for their gentle leadership to this day. The thing is that ears can only hear what they are ready for when they are ready, and I'm glad to say that I can now hear them louder and clearer than ever, even though sadly they are no longer with us physically anymore.

Not only were these two incredible warriors great role models in relation to helping me to be a strong and resilient woman, but they filled my early life with their gifts of laughter, care, and love. I can only trust I will pass this on to the next generation. This is important because women like us are the harbingers of hope and support for those coming behind us.

The point I want to make here is that understanding what shapes us enables us to identify where our patterns are playing out. This in turn enables us to dig down and identify the root cause of our behaviour and harness the power to change anything that no longer serves us.

I feel like mine is a message of hope because the reality is that nothing is set in concrete. Meanwhile, it is easy to believe that it's really hard to change. A helpful approach to take is to have the courage to change what you can, and the wisdom to know and accept what you can't.

What's very clear to me is that reviewing what's going on in our life on a regular basis is the best way to stay empowered and to consistently keep moving forward while getting closer to our highest potential.

Thoughts to Steer Your Life With

- Our values and beliefs are just a system: That said, they will rule our life if we aren't conscious of them and prepared to change anything that isn't working for us. That's why understanding where your beliefs come from and having the courage to change them is key to living a fulfilling life.

- Take a bird's eye view: When we are not so close to what's going on we can see problems from a broader perspective. This way we can see unhelpful patterns that are not serving us. What's more, with that awareness we are in a position to do something about it.

NOTES

NOTES

NOTES

NOTES

CHAPTER 6: Purpose

"Life is never made unbearable by circumstances, but only by lack of meaning and purpose"

Viktor Frankl

There is a lot of talk about finding our purpose to tap into our passion and have a meaningful life these days. It goes without saying that finding our purpose is easier if we have the equivalent of a road map that leads us to our True North. The thing is that even with a road map we can lose our way. But can we ever really be lost, or are we just on another pathway so that we can learn any lessons we need to be able to live a genuinely fulfilling life?

For many years I was a Community Worker where I was well served by my varied experience in the university of life. That armed me with the interpersonal skills and presence of mind I needed to hold a space for people who are doing it tough. I didn't need or have anything in the way of formal qualifications, but in the interest of my own personal and professional development, I decided to enrol at the Nature Care College in Sydney because they offer courses in Holistic Counselling.

That was a turning point in my life. The course that I enrolled in had a number of fantastic electives including Life Coaching, Shamanic Healing and Soul Care, as well as the core program that formed the basis of the Holistic Counselling Course I signed up for.

The first lecture I attended involved sitting in a circle with a group of about forty people. In the centre of the Circle was an exotic woven coloured rug with trinkets, ornaments, and crystals from all parts of the world on it. After the introductions and a brief explanation of how the course was going to play out, our facilitator announced that we were going to do a short guided meditation to create a sacred space in the room. As I relaxed into the meditation, I noticed the faint smell of sage and incense filling the space. With our eyes closed the room became silent as we listened to our teacher's gentle voice telling us to follow our breath going in and out in its natural flow. As I felt myself drifting off, I started to see images showing up on the wall around the room. These images were of Native American Indian Chiefs wearing a head dress of beautiful coloured feathers. They were dressed in natural brownish outfits with fringing and stitching around the sleeves, and down the side of their long brown trousers. Some had exquisite colourful beads around their necks as well.

There was a palpable sense of familiarity and power in this space. It was as if I was returning to a time I was familiar with. I felt overwhelmed as my eyes welled up with tears, then I heard my teacher's voice asking us to slowly feel ourselves coming back into the room, and to be aware of the seat we were sitting on. The images began to fade as I found myself back in the room with tears rolling down my cheeks and feeling unsure about what had happened. The teacher could see that I had been crying. After she dismissed the class for morning tea, she approached me with an expression of warmth and understanding as she explained that this can happen sometimes when people go deep into themselves. I wasn't sure how to explain what had happened, but it felt like it was something I needed to be connected to.

After everyone returned from morning tea, we had another session aimed at helping us to come back into the space with a meditation. After the deep breathing this time, I saw an image of a very big Indian Chief wearing a white breasted beaded outfit with long white trousers that had beading along the side seams. He had a real bearing and a sense of grace and honour. A young Native American girl of about eight years old with her hair in pigtails and a dress made of some kind of skin was standing in front of him this time. I couldn't see her face, but I knew and felt that it was ME!

The child spoke to the Chief (who I felt was my Grandfather) asking, "Where is my Mother?"

He said," You can't see your Mother!"

In a tearful and distressed emphatic voice I said, "I want to see my Mother!"

Suddenly there was a woman in a similar dress to the one the young child was wearing walking across the field approaching us. She was beautiful and had a colourful band around her head with a feather in it. Her young face was lovely with olive skin and big bright shiny brown eyes. I raced towards her with my arms stretched out, and wrapped my arms around her and asked, "Where have you been? I have been looking for you!"

She responded in a cool and calm voice saying, "You can't come with us."

"But I want to come with you," I said anxiously.

Then she told me that I could not go with them again in her soft, kind voice.

My Grandfather reiterated her words and then said, "You need to stay here to bring peace and harmony to the world."

At that very moment I felt a sense of relief and gratitude.

I then realized that I finally had a sense of purpose in my life. I had always felt (in this life) that I was abandoned in some way. Now I had a knowing and was able to view that from a perspective that acknowledged I had a purpose to bring harmony and peace to communities where there was none. This made my work as a Community Worker and Consultant in the present time more powerful and meaningful than ever.

After I came out of that meditation, I saw my teacher looking towards me. I sensed that she was also imbued with a knowing. She encouraged me to discuss what had happened during my experience of the meditation with the Curriculum Psychologist. They both recommended that I study Soul Care and Shamanic Healing. So I now have a Diploma in Soul Care and Shamanic Healing as well as Holistic Counselling.

This represented a massive paradigm shift for me. In fact, it was the first of many in this space of transformation and growth beyond the physical realm. Once I surrendered and gave myself permission to be who I truly and soulfully am, my life changed completely. Trusting who I was gave me a ring of confidence which enabled me to find my true identity and purpose.

The power of this experience may be difficult to comprehend as you're reading about it now. I say that because it is one of those things that needs to be experienced to be able to understand the magnitude of it. What I will say though is that it's important to be open and have the intention of connecting to our inner self on a deep level at all times.

Looking back on it now, I remember thinking that this course would be fun, but oh my goodness, it was much more than that. It was a deep, soulful experience that opened me up to doing more work on myself to make the most of my own empowerment and my ability to help others. What I want you to know is that we all have it in us to discover, explore and develop into who we really are.

Thoughts to Steer Your Life With

- Expect the unexpected: Extraordinary things happen to ordinary people when we have an open mind. It may not make sense immediately, but if you have an open mind and heart, you will always be on the right track.

- Believe in yourself: Acknowledging how wonderful you are will inevitably lead to acknowledgement coming from others.

- Have an open mind: Believing that we are all here to make a difference makes it easier for us to know and understand our purpose and the fact that opportunities to serve are unlimited.

- Be intentional: There is power in setting the intention to first find, and then stay connected to our inner soul.

NOTES

NOTES

NOTES

CHAPTER 7: Emotional Mastery

"Emotional access to the truth is the indispensable precondition of healing"

Alice Miller

I was walking along the street near one of the busiest train stations in the centre of Sydney one day when I noticed a sign for recycled clothes. I rarely see recycled clothes shops in the city, so I was interested enough to head on in and see whether there might be something there that would suit me.

I noticed there was a cardboard hand with the index finger pointing up to an unusual looking narrow escalator. I wondered if it was going to take me anywhere because it really seemed quite mysterious and as I got to the top of the first floor the lights seemed to be really dim. However, I could see that there was a small shopfront with windows surrounded with beautiful coloured bottles that captured my attention.

I felt a sense of excitement because the environment kind of captured me like a spell with the smell of sandalwood lingering in the air enticing me to enter the shop. At this stage I wasn't even sure what kind of shop it was, but the appealing entrance had a visceral impact on my body. Basically, curiosity got the better of me and I was metaphorically ushered in by a tall human size figure of an Egyptian statue that was positioned by the door. The statue with mystical eyes seemed to be watching my every move as I made my way into the shop.

Suddenly breaking my dream state and trance I heard a voice saying, "Having a nice day today?" I turned around to see a woman who was probably in her mid-50s dressed elegantly in a long purple skirt and a bright hot pink scarf draped around her neck. She had long white hair in a bun, hazel eyes, and red lipstick that highlighted her smile.

I stumbled over my words, but managed to get out, "So what are these beautiful coloured bottles? They are absolutely amazing! I have never seen anything like them before."

The woman introduced herself. "I'm Roxanna, and I am a Practitioner for Aura Soma." Hers was an accent I wasn't familiar with, so it made the experience of interacting with her all the more interesting. Aura-Soma means etheric body-physical body. The etheric body, or aura, is an electromagnetic field that clairvoyants see as coloured rays emanating from the spine of the person they're communicating with.

As we know, colours are simply wavelengths of light. But what most people don't know is that we are actually made of light ourselves. As such, our own true vibration is mirrored in various frequencies of colour. So when I chose colours from among the Equilibrium bottles that were in the shop for example, I was attracted to them because those particular colours 'spoke' to me, and I got that it was my job to understand what they wanted to tell me.

The thing is that in bringing the colours we choose from the Equilibrium bottles into our etheric body, we are not only re-establishing our aura to its natural rainbow, but also bringing balance to the aura and to the even-more-refined bodies that make up the totality of our light body. So, in a sense, the Equilibrium colours are simply bringing us into the light of our own true colours.

Roxanna went on to explain how the Aura Soma products could help people to heal.

What she said was that "In alternative healing, imbalances are understood to have been caused by the way we respond to emotions with thoughts and decisions that have essentially altered our deepest essence. When we utilise the power of colour through the Equilibrium bottles, we synchronize their wavelengths to our body's electromagnetic field, harmonizing any imbalances. Unlike most therapies, in which the therapist chooses the healing substance, Aura-Soma is totally and almost uniquely non-intrusive. For it is you who seeks healing and chooses your own colours. This is important because it strengthens your bond to the Great Healer that you carry inside yourself. When you can stop the chattering of the conscious mind and go into the silence, this inner healer, our Higher Self, knows what the right thing is for you, and always chooses wisely. I believe that we can truly say that Aura-Soma is a powerful method of self healing."

Roxanna smiled again with her caring and reassuring yet so professional manner as she advised me to choose my colours from the selection of bottles. She said to choose them intuitively and explained what the colours I had chosen signified.

- Orange represented the binary opposites of Independence/dependency with reference to shock, trauma, deep insight and bliss.

- Turquoise represented media/group communication, and communicating creatively through art.

- Magenta represented love for the little things in daily life.

I was incredibly grateful to Roxanna because the information she shared gave a new sense of meaning to my life, and an awareness of the emotions the various colours represent.

What the Aura-Soma Colours Mean

Red: Energy, grounding, survival issues and the material side of life.

Coral: Unrequited love.

Orange: Independence/dependency, shock, trauma, deep insight and bliss.

Gold: Wisdom and intense fear.

Yellow: Acquired knowledge.

Olive: Creating a space for clarity and wisdom.

Green: Space. Search for truth. Panoramic consciousness.

Turquoise: Mass media/group communication. Creative Communication (art).

Blue: Peace and communication.

Royal blue: Knowing why one is here.

Violet: Spirituality, healing, serving others.

Magenta: Love for the little things in daily life.

Pink: Unconditional love and caring.

Clear (white): Suffering and the understanding of suffering.

Thoughts to Steer Your Life With

- Strive for Emotional mastery: This is the process of attaining complete emotional control. When we have the ability to do this, we will experience better relationships with ourselves and others, as well as improved wellbeing both physically and mentally.

- Consider and acknowledge our emotions: It's easier to find solutions to the why and the what in relation to triggering emotions when we respond to the situation with curiosity.

- Things happen for a reason: The best way to work out what the reason is, is by trusting your own intuition.

- Strive to hone your skills in understanding your emotional state: Even though I had done a lot of work on myself before finding out about the Aura-Soma approach, my emotional life still had its fair share of chaos. However, now that the other work I've done is being reinforced by the Aura-Soma products, I have a deeper level of understanding of my emotional state which gives me a lot more insight into what's going on at any given time.

- Give yourself permission to BE in the moment and go with the Flow: If you do this often enough it will become your default state, and you will have completely transformed your life and the energy you show up with on a day to day basis.

NOTES

NOTES

NOTES

CHAPTER 8: Fun and Travel

"Life is either a daring adventure or nothing at all"

Helen Keller

I left home with one backpack when I went to France in 1999. I had one book in my backpack. It was "The Art of Happiness" by the Dalai Lama. Reading that book was like listening to a conversation between the Dalai Lama and another scholar called Dr Howard Cutler. For some reason, I believed this was the best book to have as my companion on my travels where I was expecting to have some wonderful adventures. It was appropriate because I had set an intention to meditate and be mindful on my trip.

I was leaving a very stressful job and determined to leave that kind of life behind me. I was so stressed that I actually developed alopecia areata. My mission was to find space where I could be myself without the pressure of family and relationships. If I needed any proof that this was the right way to go, I got it in the form of my hair growing back after I'd been living in Paris for eighteen months.

Another thing I was committed to doing was the exercises I had learned from Falun Gong. These are similar to Tai Chi exercises. The original process of exercise in China is Qigong. I focus on this now after many years of practice. What I found out while I was travelling is that these two practices were both banned in China. I really love them because they give me a sense of peace and harmony. They also reminded me to appreciate the freedom I had while I was travelling on my own, as a free spirit making choices that supported me. I knew that I was damn lucky to be in the position I was in where I could follow my passion with curiosity and commitment. I felt overwhelmed with joy and full of gratitude at the time.

My intention was to go to Barcelona on the other side of the world to teach English. I had a one year around the world ticket that meant I could travel in and out of any country as long as I wasn't altering the direction I was travelling in. I was attracted to Barcelona because I had a work colleague from Australia who was also there and offered to help me find networks over there. Unfortunately, things didn't go to plan. After a week staying in a lovely little cheap boutique hotel my money was running out and my friend never contacted me. So I moved on to plan B with Einstein's quote "In the middle of difficulty lies opportunity" ringing in my ears. Plan B involved moving on. I had one other address from another work colleague who had offered to connect me with a good friend in Paris.

I thought I might as well go to Paris because there was nothing really on offer for me in Spain. So I checked the options out and found that the cheapest way to travel from Barcelona to the centre of Paris was by an overnight train. With my heavy backpack and a small package of food I found myself in a cabin with two bunks that was reasonably clean. No-one was there so I thought I was in luck and had a cabin to myself. I waited and waited, then I heard the stationmaster calling out "All aboard!" and we were off. I climbed up to the top bunk and felt like a teenager again on an adventure to an unknown place. I smiled to myself and thought, "Hey, this is the life!"

The train puffed along with the sun setting as I looked out the window. It was still light enough to see as we passed a little village with quaint colourful houses looking like a small toy land village. It was the kind of place where I wouldn't have been surprised to have seen Noddy getting out of his little car. We crossed the old wooden bridge on my journey to another part of the world. I had settled in for the night when I heard the train come to a standstill. That's when I realised I must have been asleep as I'd woken with the sound of the rhythm of the wheels on the tracks making a kind of droning sound that had sent me off to sleep some time earlier.

I heard a few voices, and what I thought sounded like a couple of small dogs. I looked down over to the side of my bunk and saw a woman settling in with two small tan coloured Pomeranians in the cabin I was in. Oh no, so much for quiet time on my own. I lay half-awake/half-asleep not even trying to sleep when I suddenly found myself rubbing my eyes with the light of the sun coming up. I had almost forgotten where I was. I looked down and saw the two small dogs lying down under the bottom bunk. The woman looked up and said with a French accent, "So sorry, I hope the dogs didn't wake you." I let her know that I didn't hear them at all. I was actually feeling a little guilty about being so judgemental when I first saw them.

When we pulled into Chatelet station in Paris I grabbed my bag and got off the train. I was surrounded by people with heavy suitcases and came to the conclusion that this wasn't going to be just a holiday. It was full of a sense of mysteriousness. Paris felt like a magical place with its beautiful language and culture. My excitement rose and I had a huge smile on my face when I realised that without even trying, I was open to whatever was going to come my way. I was leaning into self leadership at its best and totally trusting my intuition at that point.

Thoughts to Steer Your Life With

- Keep it short and simple: You are much less likely to be disappointed if you don't overcomplicate things and have no expectations.

- Travel with curiosity: Moving around with enthusiasm and zest for a positive outcome will make your life infinitely more easeful.

- Follow your intuition: Seek answers from within rather than always turning to external sources for validation.

- Surrender and say yes to opportunities that come your way.

NOTES

NOTES

NOTES

NOTES

CHAPTER 9: Self Leadership

"Personal Leadership is the process of keeping your vision and values before you and aligning your life to be congruent with them"

Stephen Covey

I wish I knew then what I know now.

It all began when I was just five years old taking the tiny steps that I mentioned at the beginning of the book when I used the words 'leaving my mum's apron's strings'. Little did I know at the time that this was the door opening to a journey that was full of exploration and discovery around the way my life's plan was to unfold. Of course, that entailed getting ready to leave my 'safe haven' which was a busy Chinese household with six girls and plenty of aromatic smells coming from the delicious food I grew up with.

My dad's special recipe of fresh chicken soup with Chinese herbs boiling on a Saturday morning often comes back to mind. Even though we were poor we never skimped on food. The mantra in our house was to eat well to stay strong. My parents were always making sure that we ate even if we weren't hungry. Yet for some reason we were always hungry as kids.

I remember feeling safe and embraced by the comfort food that still spells family to me. My mum and dad always seem to be preparing food. My dad was a cook in the American Air Force and seemed to always be cooking for the troops in our tiny kitchen where we had a big double gas wok set up. Dad somehow managed to always churn out stunning 'soong' which is a selection of food that feels like a banquet.

Our house was very simple. It was in the inner city of Sydney where real estate prices have gone through the roof to the extent that families like the one I grew up in would never be able to afford these days. But in the early 50s when I was growing up it was one of the slum areas of Sydney. Our place had a reasonably sized room that was set up as a kitchen and laundry with a copper that was concreted into a corner of the room. The bathroom was partitioned off from the kitchen. It was basically a peeling old bathtub with two taps, with only the cold water working. It trickled slowly out of the tap because the water pressure was so weak. There was no hand basin, so we washed our hands over the bath. The bathroom/kitchen didn't have hot water until I was at high school, and we had an outside toilet.

Regardless of the condition of the house and the fact that it was deep within the working-class area of Sydney, it was our cosy two-bedroom home filled with luscious food made with love and care that fills me with a feeling of warmth and security even as I think about it now. I believe it's true that home is where the heart is.

Anyone who visited us (whether it was one of my mum's seven brothers, or my dad's friend visiting from China on the merchant ships, or our local neighbours) were embraced and felt like they were welcome to join us in our cosy home at any time of the day or night. Our home had the values of Confucius embedded in it thanks to my quiet but authoritarian father. Meanwhile, Mum's warm heart gave us the connections and socialisation skills that set us up well to have a good life full of lovely friends. We never had any reason to doubt that they had our wellbeing at heart. If only the 'outside world' followed suit!

We had Chinese names given to us at birth. These weren't on our birth certificates though. Except in the case of my older sister Meilaan, we were all called by our English names that ended with 'lan' (meaning the orchid flower). The assumption was that we would turn out to be pretty, smiling, happy, laughing little flowers in human form.

A sad thing that happened when I was still very young is that the sister who came along after me passed away. We believed this happened because Dad had wanted a boy after having three girls and broke the pattern of using 'Lan' at the end of her name. Names are important in Chinese culture, and Chinese superstition suggests that breaking the convention like my father did explains why we lost our sister. It was as if my father's actions brought bad luck to our family. Whether there's any veracity in that idea or not, the way things panned out dramatically aged my father.

It was only in later years that it occurred to me that the stress of losing my younger sister at the age of three, and the way I resorted to grieving internally would have added significantly to the stress I was living with from a young age. No one at the time ever asked me how I felt, so I never discussed it, but internally and externally I have always acknowledged her absence.

Looking outwardly rather than inwardly wasn't easy for me. In fact, I had no choice but to go inward because I was plagued with angst, pain and depression when I was young. Basically, I felt misunderstood because I didn't fit neatly into any role and didn't seem to be able to live up to other people's expectations.

My upbringing was focussed on not creating problems and fitting right into the Western model of operating and assimilating with the people around us. My mum would say, "You'll be fine", or "They don't mean it", whenever I told her about children at school who were bullying me or making racist remarks. Whether they meant it or not, it was still hurtful to be in this challenging environment where I felt invisible and as if I didn't count.

There were times when it definitely mattered though. For example, once my teacher insisted that I had to dance with one of the two Chinese boys in my class. This just felt unfair and like discrimination to me. Meanwhile, my understanding was that from my family's perspective, I was meant to be accommodating. I was often told to be the 'good Chinese girl' who doesn't make waves and is always considerate of others. I did all of that, but I still lived in a toxic emotional soup of **FEAR** and **STRESS** about getting it wrong.

It was very difficult to fit into any of the 'groups' at the all-girl high school that I attended. There were the Malaysian Chinese group, and another one for people from Hong Kong, but no Australian Born Chinese students like me. Needless to say, I certainly didn't relate to the Anglo Saxon or Jewish groups either. The result was that I had no sense of belonging and continued to suffer from anxiety and stress all through my school years. I barely made it to school for the minimum days required to obtain my School Certificate. When my teacher noticed how irregular my attendance was, she asked me about it. I told her that I had trouble getting up to come to school. To my surprise she said, "Just come when you can." Her acknowledgment made me feel like someone noticed whether I was there or not.

Things came to a head when I had a nervous breakdown. It was terrible at the time, but in hindsight it's clear that it represented a turning point for me. I say that because in my darkest hour I got to see that owning my identity as a young Chinese woman living in Australia meant that I had the best of both worlds. That realisation set me free from feeling like a victim who didn't belong.

The journey of discovery and exploration of my inner world still continues. I've had the opportunity to work in the multicultural and diversity sector as a Migrant Child Worker, Community Development Worker and Diversity Health Coordinator for many years. Blowing the trumpet for the cause of social justice and the rights of people from all races, genders and socio-economic backgrounds is an obsession for me.

Why wouldn't it be? I feel blessed to continue my journey with all the wisdom and courage that I've learned along the way.

The bottom line is that empowering others is what I choose to do through my work as an Integrative Life Coach. This is what I've been put on this earth for. As far as I'm concerned, no one needs to have a life of stress and/or anxiety if they are prepared to do the work to transcend unhelpful conditioning and outdated patterns that no longer serve them. I believe that it is my life purpose to bring **PEACE** and **HARMONY** to the World by being the best version of myself and helping others to do the same.

Thoughts to Steer Your Life With

- Be your own person: Finding your own journey and purpose is the only way to lead a truly fulfilling life.

- Cultivate self awareness: Understanding your own values and beliefs is the key to achieving your potential.

- Be grateful for everyone and everything that comes your way: Sometimes we find it hard to understand the point of difficult situations when they present themselves, but on reflection the purpose is usually revealed if we maintain a high level of self awareness.

NOTES

NOTES

NOTES

NOTES

CHAPTER 10: Relationships

"You'll know when a relationship is right for you. It will enhance your life, not complicate your life"

Brigitte Nicole

As I reflect on the relationships that came my way over the years (and I am sure there are more to come), I can see that having robust supportive relationships is just as important as eating high quality healthy food. I remember imagining having a boyfriend at the age of five. In fact, it feels like being in love was always central to my heart's desire.

I liked having male company and good conversations at primary school. Going to an all-girl high school really dampened my social life. I always seemed to be playing the role of the big sister or the open minded, non-judgemental female that males needed to have around for reassurance. So, I would often be chatting to the males at the local Chinese dances we attended in our teens, while other couples would be smooching during the last dance with the slow music, as I was sharing jokes with the males who didn't get to find their date for the night.

Unfortunately, I realised early in life that I was at odds with the agenda of the males (and many of the females) I was growing up around, and in one case, actually married.

Things changed as my horizons broadened after I was divorced. I transformed myself from being a suburban housewife to becoming the Manager of a Zulu dancer and singer. This gave me an opportunity to see very different kinds of lives that I would never have even known existed if I'd still been married and living in the suburbs.

On one occasion for example, I was volunteering for an African event being held in Canberra. The whole long weekend was full of African music and cultural activities. I knew an African Zulu singer living in Sydney who was performing with a band of musicians including a French-Caribbean bass guitarist. I was mingling with the other band members when I first saw the tall French-Caribbean man who was to play a part in my becoming the woman I am today. I could see that he was a man of style with his tidy long dreaded hair. He was dressed in a smart tailored jacket and flattering dark trousers. The whole outfit showed up his suaveness and chicness. That quality combined with his big dark eyes and a sweet kind of shyness made him very appealing to me. He was obviously attracted to me as well because he smiled and said, "Vous etes belle" to his friend as he was looking my way.

One of the band members who spoke French and English asked me whether I understood what he was saying about me. My French wasn't that good, and I was feeling a bit coy, so I responded, "No, not really." He then went on to tell me that his friend had said that I'm beautiful. Wow! My body was feeling warm, and I humbly thanked him by saying, "Really, Merci Beaucoup." Inside my heart was racing with excitement while my mind was telling me that he was just being a typical flirtatious French male. I guess I felt vulnerable yet flattered.

During the day I saw him quietly standing by himself, so I called him over. I wanted him to feel welcome because I know that sometimes in Australia responses to people from other cultures are not always as welcoming as they could be. I managed to converse with him really well because we had a great rapport. Among other things we found that we both liked eating healthily, and had the same music tastes, family values and beliefs.

He was born and bred in Paris, but his ethnicity is Caribbean because his family hails from Martinique in the Caribbean Islands. He asked me to meet him later that night after he finished playing at his gig. The organisers had set up a nightclub where we met later and had a great conversation and danced for a while before I drove him back to his hotel. Our ability to really communicate with each other was amazing. It just flowed and brought us together way beyond the depth of the physical connection we made. He was very keen to meet up the next day, so we met up as planned. I found this to be a bit unusual to be honest. I guess having worked with musicians and other creative groups from other cultural backgrounds had conditioned me to expect uncertainty because they tended to be a little 'unaware' of time and sometimes a bit unreliable.

Cultural differences and similarities made our friendship and relationship colourful and exciting. It continued for many years and is one of the relationships that was particularly significant to my development and growth. That's not because it was full of romance - far from it. My sense of it is that it was the challenges and the chaos, as well as the love in between that made the growth I went through particularly deep. At the end of the day, it was the fact that we were soul mates with a bit of karma thrown in that made it part of the journey I was destined to venture into and come out the other side.

At times it was painful and yet I had a real sense of becoming stronger. I will always be grateful for this. On a side note, he also fathered two children with another woman in Australia while he was with me. I feel like this is significant in the context of the fact that the idea of a love triangle has always been present in my life. I was once told I was the concubine of a King in a past life. A feeling of familiarity with this pattern played out until I learnt to 'let that go' in later life as it no longer served me.

The thing is that patterns will show up in many forms during our life. Self awareness makes it easier for us to address the complexities involved in living, and it also guides us through the tunnel that must be ventured in to so that we can come out the other side. After being married for twenty years and having three children, I went on to have casual relationships and friendships, as well as life changing experiences with two other younger men. These relationships resulted in my gaining courage and wisdom. Then when I was feeling very comfortable, I connected with an older man with narcissistic tendencies. Of course, I didn't realise that was the case until it was too late. I was hoping that this relationship would be more stabilizing than the previous ones, but unfortunately that wasn't how it turned out.

Needless to say, this wasn't fun. In fact, it was really hard, but in hindsight I'm grateful for the lessons I learned and the things I discovered about myself and the ongoing development that life is all about. It's relationships like this one that have provided the impetus for change in my life. They have helped me build resilience as I continue to evolve and become the best version of ME I can possibly be. Perhaps one of the most significant lessons I've learnt is the importance of taking responsibility for the outcomes of the choices I make.

One of the most important things I realised some years ago was that my habit of blaming myself for anything that didn't work out, and positioning myself in stressful situations in relation to the personal and professional aspects of my life, probably explains my developing male baldness alopecia many years ago. I wore a wig most of the time back then, however, there was a part of me that couldn't feel truly comfortable not showing up as myself. That said, wearing a wig was the choice I made at the time, and I honour myself for that. Just as I honour myself more recently for shaving my head because I feel liberated this way now.

I've also learnt that the relationships we have with ourselves and others can be seen as a kind of 'gift' of torment that we get when we work with a really tough mentor. For example, in hindsight I can see that the incredibly challenging time I had at school was a lesson in disguise, because some of the most important lessons life has for us can only be learned through the experience of pain and discomfort. I can honestly say that every bit of learning I've had to this day has given me a sense of achievement, as well as raising my confidence and increasing clarity around what matters to me.

I say these things with sincerity and honesty because once we realise that life is about learning while living authentically and consciously, it's easy to see it as a journey to be lived with enthusiasm and curiosity. When we approach life that way, we will have a sense of appreciation or possibly even gratitude for whatever happens, safe in the knowledge that the sun slowly sets every day and the moon shines at night regardless of the dramas we might be going through at any given time.

I'm in a place now where I make my way through the good times and the tough times in a state of wonderment. I've learnt that resisting what might be going on is more painful than dealing with the trials and tribulations that are a part of learning and growing. 'Go with the flow' is my motto these days.

This book is my challenge to you to look beyond everyday existence and trust that there is more to life than what you see on the surface. So the journey continues, and I would love to invite you to come along on it with me.

Thoughts to Steer Your Life With

- Learn to be assertive: Combining assertiveness with an understanding of what lies behind our responses, reactions and other behaviours is an empowered way to go about life.

- Be open and non-judgmental in relation to yourself and others: This is the best way to establish solid relationships.

- Have integrity: This involves not only being honest with others, it also entails being honest with yourself.

- Have boundaries: This is key to having a fulfilling life.

- Prioritise self care: This is about knowing your own needs and responding accordingly

- Be open to opportunities: This is not only about not closing yourself down. It also includes being open to seeing everything that comes your way as opportunities.

- Spend a lot of time out of your comfort zone. This is the only way to feel truly alive.

- Have gratitude: Show kindness to yourself and others and be heart-centred in all that you do.

NOTES

NOTES

NOTES

NOTES

CONCLUSION

I hope you've taken time to reflect on your own situation as you've read about what's got me to where I am now. I say that because while most of the content in this book is about me, you're actually the most important person in this scenario.

I've shared what I've included in the chapters you've read so that you might gain a sense of peace in the knowledge that no matter how tough life might be from time to time, there is value in learning the lessons that are in the difficult experiences that life is likely to throw our way.

I want to congratulate you for making your way to the end of this book. What you might like to do now is copy whatever you've found useful in the "Thoughts to Steer Your Life With" sections at the end of each chapter and add some dot points of your own. It's a great idea to have that list handy whenever you feel like you're on the precipice of growth. You'll know you're there whenever the level of stress and discomfort you're feeling seems to be pushing you to your limits. We don't get to that point because we're about to break down. We get there because we're actually about to break through to a space on a whole other level if we play our cards right.

REFERENCE

Working with Emotional Intelligence, Edition 1, Coleman, Daniel (1999). Bloomsbury.

Search Inside Yourself: The unexpected Path to Achieving Success, Happiness and World Peace, Meng Tan, Chade (2014). Harper San Francisco.

The Hidden Power of Emotional Intuition, Mendoza, Maya Vega (2002). Pavilion Books.

The Habits of Highly Effective People Stephen R Covey, 2020 Series: The Covey Habits Series. Simon and Schuster Australia.

The Courage to Change: Living the 7 Habits Covey, Stephen R (1995). Free Press.

Secrets of Natural Success - Five Steps to Unlocking Your Genius, Writecloud, William (2019). Animal Dreaming Publishing.

ABOUT THE AUTHOR

Saulan is an Integrative Life Coach for the Mind, Body and Spirit who incorporates complementary therapies with the *Transform Yourself in Five Simple Steps* program that she developed to ensure that her clients get from where they are to where they want to be.

Her own background of growing up as a Chinese woman who was born in Australia gave her a passion for cultural diversity and working tirelessly for human rights and social justice.

Saulan is a lifelong learner who has achieved a number of qualifications including a Bachelor of Arts degree and a Diploma in Soul Care Shamanic Healing.

Some of the other studies Saulan has participated in include:

- Cross Cultural Training.
- Leadership in High Stress Workplaces.
- Coaching Psychology.
- Holistic Counselling.
- Diversity Management Leadership.
- Pay it Forward Community Leadership.
- Facilitator and Parenting Education.

In addition to one-on-one coaching, Saulan also conducts workshops on the themes of Change, Resilience and Emotional Mastery.

Saulan has been featured in a number of other books including:

- Legacies for a Better World: Seniors on Sustainability. Randwick Council 2010.

- Words of Wisdom: Celebrating the Seniors of Randwick City. Randwick Council 2017.

- Stories from the Street. Randwick Council 2018.

- Undefeated: 90 Migrant Women 118 Journeys. A Professional Migrant Women Project. 2022

You can contact Saulan at: https://authenticconsciousliving.com.au/ and E: yinlosaulan@gmail.com

www.ingramcontent.com/pod-product-compliance
Lightning Source LLC
Chambersburg PA
CBHW030301010526
44107CB00053B/1771